the Great Wall
of China

Kerri O'Donnell

The Rosen Publishing Group's

READING ROOM

New York

Published in 2003 by The Rosen Publishing Group, Inc.
29 East 21st Street, New York, NY 10010

Book Design: Michael Flynn

Photo Credits: Cover, p. 1 © Pete Turner/Image Bank; p. 7 (satellite image of Great Wall) © Photo Disc; pp. 8 (both images), 16–17 © Dean Conger/Corbis; pp. 10–11 (background) © SuperStock; p. 11 (emperor) © Charles & Josette Lenars/Corbis; p. 12 © North Wind Pictures; p. 15 © Andy Caulfield/Image Bank; pp. 18–19 © Image Bank; p. 20 (cannons) © Wolfgang Kaehler/Corbis; p. 20 (forts) © Image Bank; p. 22 © Steve Vidler/SuperStock.

Library of Congress Cataloging-in-Publication Data

O'Donnell, Kerri.
  The Great Wall of China / Kerri O'Donnell.
      p. cm. — (Rosen Publishing Group's reading room collection)
  ISBN 0-8239-3715-1
  1. Great Wall of China (China—Juvenile literature. I. Title. II.
Series.
  DS793.G67 O35 2003
  951—dc21

                              2001007684

Manufactured in the United States of America

For More Information
The Great Wall of China—Enchanted Learning
http://www.enchantedlearning.com/subjects/greatwall/

China: Dim Sum: Great Wall of China Photographs
http://www.newton.mec.edu/Angier/DimSum/Great%20Wall%20Pix.html

 # Contents

China

About one in every five people
on Earth lives in China!

長城長城　長城長城

 China at a Glance

China is a very large country in the eastern part of Asia. Asia is the largest **continent** in the world. China's land covers more than one-fifth of Asia. Russia and Canada are the only countries on Earth that are bigger than China. China is made up of farmland, tall mountains, and deserts.

China also has one of the longest rivers in the world, the Yangtze (YANG-SEE). The Yangtze is more than 3,900 miles long!

A Great Wall

The Great Wall of China is the longest **structure** ever built on Earth. The Great Wall is about 4,500 miles long and was built completely by hand. It crosses the northern part of China, from the eastern coast to the north-central part of the country.

In the east, the Great Wall winds its way through tall mountains. Farther west, the Great Wall winds through lower, flatter areas and China's **Gobi Desert**.

The Great Wall of China is so large that it can be seen from space!

Great Wall

China

Great Wall

The Great Wall Through Time

China's written history goes back about 3,500 years. Written records tell us that the Chinese probably began building the Great Wall in the seventh century B.C. That's about 2,600 years ago! Building of the wall probably ended in the 1500s. The Great Wall is actually made up of many different walls that were connected to each other at different times in China's history.

Different groups of people in China built walls to keep enemies out of their land and keep themselves safe.

★ People Power

In 221 B.C., different states that had been at war with each other were **united** to form China. The next fifteen years were known as the Qin (CHIN) **dynasty**. During this time, the ruler of China had his people begin building a "great" wall by connecting new walls with older ones. This wall was called the Qin Wall and was about 3,000 miles long. It took over 3 million people to build the wall. That was almost three-fourths of the entire population of China at that time!

The man shown here was the first ruler of united China. He ordered the first "Great Wall" to be built.

長城長城

長城長城

12

Building the Wall

From around 202 B.C. to 220 A.D., the Han dynasty ruled much of the land that we now call China. During this time, workers built about 300 miles of new wall. This extended the wall through the Gobi Desert in the west. Brick and stone were not easy to find in the western lands. Instead, workers used wet earth, stone, and branches to build the wall. When the wet earth dried, the wall became solid and strong.

Roads along the Great Wall made it possible for people to trade valuable things like horses, spices, and silk with western lands. These roads were called the "Silk Roads."

The Ming Wall

The main part of the Great Wall is called the Ming Wall. It is located in eastern China. The Ming Wall was built during the Ming dynasty, which lasted from 1368 to 1644. The part of the Great Wall we see today is mostly from this period in China's history.

The Ming Wall is about 2,150 miles long. It has a base of **granite** blocks. The sides are made of stone or brick. The top of the wall is a brick road.

Workers used the road on top of the Great Wall to carry supplies. Soldiers used the road to keep the wall safe from enemies.

★ ✦ Strengthening the Wall

During the Ming dynasty, workers fixed and strengthened much of the brick and granite from hundreds of years before, which were falling apart. The wall's towers were also fixed and strengthened. This was done to keep away enemies from the north.

The Ming Wall ranges from fifteen to thirty feet high and from fifteen to twenty-five feet wide. A road on top of the wall averages about thirteen feet wide.

Even today, workers continue to fix and strengthen parts of the Great Wall.

The Chinese people used the wall to send messages to each other about their enemies. Guards on the wall could see their enemies from many miles away. The guards would then burn wood and straw to warn people of possible danger. One **column** of smoke meant that an enemy army of less than 500 men was heading for the wall. Four columns of smoke meant that an army of up to 10,000 men was approaching the wall!

長城長城

長城長城

At one time, the Ming Wall was guarded by more than a million men!

Defending the Wall

Towns and **forts** along the Ming Wall served as headquarters for troops of soldiers. People in each tower along the wall had a different job to do and could pass messages down the entire length of the wall. This way, the rulers of the country could stay in touch with the soldiers and **defend** the country.

Some of the forts along the Ming Wall are less than 200 feet apart. Soldiers in these forts could watch for enemies and shoot at them with **cannons**.

During the Ming Dynasty, thousands of forts were built to defend the wall.

The Great Wall Today

In the centuries since the Ming dynasty, a lot of the Great Wall has fallen apart. In 1949, China began rebuilding parts of the wall. Today, many people from all over the world come to China to see the Great Wall. It is an excellent example of the history of Chinese **civilization**.

 **Glossary**

cannon   A very large gun that fires over long distances.

civilization   A way of life followed by the people of a certain time and place.

column   Something with a tall, thin shape.

continent   One of the seven large areas of land on Earth.

defend   To keep something safe from enemies.

dynasty   A line of rulers who belong to the same family.

fort   A strong building used by soldiers to defend a place.

Gobi Desert   A desert in Asia. Part of the Gobi Desert is in western China.

granite   A very hard rock that is often used in building.

structure   Something that is built.

united   Joined together as a single group.

⭐ Index